Teachers and You

LEVEL 6
/e_e/ea/

DECODABLES
BY jump!

Teaching Tips

Orange Level 6

This book focuses on the phonemes **/e_e /ea /**.

Before Reading

- Discuss the title. Ask readers what they think the book will be about. Have them briefly explain why.
- Remind readers of the book's focused phonics phonemes. What do they notice about the "e" sound in these phonemes? Are they long or short vowel sounds?

Read the Book

- Encourage readers to break down unfamiliar words into units of sound. Then, ask them to string the sounds together to create the words.
- Urge readers to point out when the focused phonics phonemes appear in the text.

After Reading

- Encourage children to reread the book independently or with a friend.
- Ask readers to name other words with /e_e/ or /ea/ phonemes. On a separate sheet of paper, have them write the words.

© 2024 Booklife Publishing
This edition is published by arrangement with Booklife Publishing.

North American adaptations © 2024 Jump!
5357 Penn Avenue South
Minneapolis, MN 55419
www.jumplibrary.com

Decodables by Jump! are published by Jump! Library.
All rights reserved. No part of this book may be reproduced in any form without written permission from the publisher.

Library of Congress Cataloging-in-Publication Data is available at www.loc.gov or upon request from the publisher.

ISBN: 979-8-88524-763-4 (hardcover)
ISBN: 979-8-88524-764-1 (paperback)
ISBN: 979-8-88524-765-8 (ebook)

How many kinds of teachers can you name?

Good morning! Take a seat, and we will start the lesson. I am a math teacher. Let's get to it!

A math teacher will teach you math. Math is all about numbers and solving. Math teachers can help you complete hard problems.

I am an art teacher. Art is how we express what we think and feel. It might be with a painting or a drawing.

An art teacher might help us gain skills, such as new ways to paint.

This is a painting of a beach.

Can you play an instrument? I can help teach you how to play one. Let's play the drums.

A drum teacher can help you play the beat to a song. To get good at the drums, you must repeat a beat lots and lots.

I am a swimming teacher. Swimming is a sport that is good for you. It can help keep you safe in the sea too.

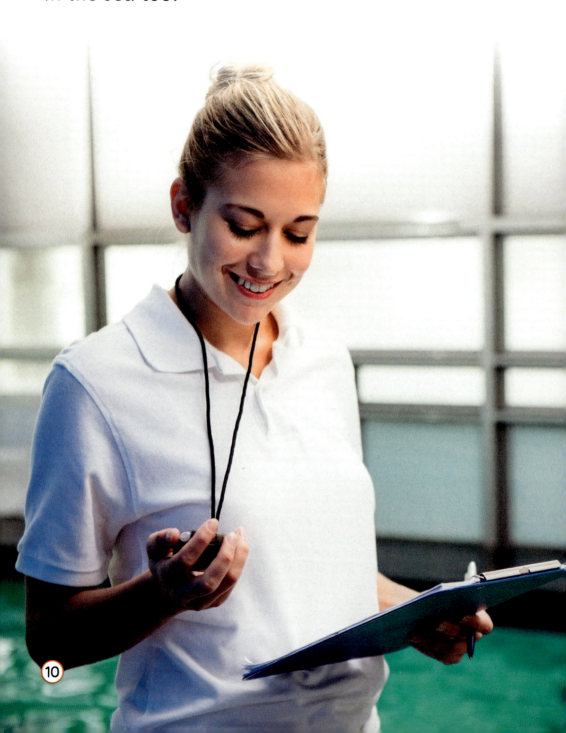

A swimming teacher can help you compete against kids just like you. They can even help you turn into an athlete!

I am an acting coach. I can teach you how to be in a play or a film!

In an acting lesson, the acting coach might set a theme that you need to act out, or you may have a script to read.

I can teach you lots of skills for when you are out in the forest. I can teach you how to camp in the woods.

An outdoors teacher can teach you how to have fun and stay safe in extreme settings.

Teachers help us gain skills that we keep forever.

Can you name the missing letters for each word?

b _ _ _ ds

_ _v _ _ning

dr _ _ _ _m